Postcards

A Collector's Guide

Postcards

A Collector's Guide

Chris Connor

MILLER'S POSTCARDS: A COLLECTOR'S GUIDE
by Chris Connor

First published in Great Britain in 2000 by Miller's, a division of
Mitchell Beazley, imprints of Octopus Publishing Group Ltd,
2–4 Heron Quays, London E14 4JP

Miller's is a registered trademark of Octopus Publishing Group Ltd

Commissioning Editor **Anna Sanderson**
Executive Art Editor **Vivienne Brar**
Editors **Selina Mumford & Samantha Ward-Dutton**
Designer **Louise Griffiths**
Indexer **Sue Farr**
Proofreader **Laura Hicks**
Picture Research **Helen Stallion**
Production **Jessame Emms**
Specially commissioned photography by **A. J. Photographics
& Steve Tanner**
Jacket photograph by **Steve Tanner**

ISBN 1 84000 190 9
A CIP record for this book is available from the British Library
Set in Bembo, Frutiger, and Shannon
Produced by Toppan Printing Co., (HK) Ltd.
Printed and bound in China

Jacket illustrations, clockwise from top: A sailor and his lover, part of a
romantic series, c.1925; "God Jul" (A Happy Christmas and New Year),
Swedish, c.1900; "To My Valentine", c.1909; "Etoile d'Amour", 1913;
A butterfly, Alpha novelty card, c.1910

SHE
LOVES
ME.

SHE
LOVES ME
NOT.

contents

The origin of the postcard

Almost everyone bought and sent cards compulsively at the peak of the postcard craze in 1903. Every corner shop or stall sold them, and the demand for novelty and variety was enormous. Postcards were a rapid and amusing means of communication, and with six or seven postal deliveries a day in cities, people could make an appointment with certainty for later that same day. Small talk, gossip, holiday messages, and even romances were pursued on cards. Albums filled with cards provided entertainment for families and friends. Local photographers recorded accidents and events, and stage artists used cards to publicize their shows.

So what triggered this explosion of print and is it relevant today? In 1802, on a wave of reform, the Factory Act was passed in Britain.

Significantly, this ensured that child labourers had a basic education. The effects were profound, and, as similar measures were brought in throughout the industrialized world, adult literacy blossomed. By 1840 a generation of literate people could communicate by writing, and this at a time when the Industrial Revolution was splitting families and creating new urban communities. The Penny Post was created in Britain to cater for this growing market.

In 1869 Dr Emmanuel Hermann persuaded the Austrian Postal Authorities to accept his small, thin, buff card, with the address and an embossed, engraved stamp on one side and space for a message on the reverse. In 1870 the British and Swiss Postal Authorities accepted a similar design.

The postal card was conceived for business purposes, to confirm orders, deliveries, and receipts, and to act as a reminder, and was accepted and collected as part of the philatelic tradition. In Europe, however, the message side also carried an illustration, and these became increasingly elaborate and colourful. A new chromolithographic printing process which enabled cheaper colour printing developed in Prussia and Saxony during this period, and these cards excited much interest among the public. In 1894 publishers finally gained the right to print their own postcards, but these

View from Decorative Arts Palace, Franco-British Exhibition, London, 1908

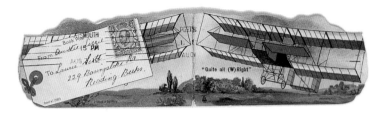

"court cards" were narrower than the Continental cards. The bigger images and extra message space of the latter were still more popular. Adolph Tuck of Messrs Raphael Tuck & Sons, one of Britain's best known greetings-card publishers, campaigned successfully to get the Post Office to accept the larger format of its European competitors.

When postcards first appeared, they were mocked as being fit only for the illiterate and vulgar, reflecting Victorian attitudes. Nevertheless, society was changing, and even members of the Royal Family used and collected postcards. The Prime Minister corresponded on postcards, and writers such as Bernard Shaw advocated their use. The final significant design modification came in 1904, when the European Postal Union accepted the "divided back" for cards: the address was to be written on the right and a message on the left with a line separating them. This freed the image side completely and produced the format we know today. The astronomical sales of cards

continued until the outbreak of World War I, when the public mood changed, and the collecting of cards became much less popular. Card sales fell, but their diversity was retained.

Today the useful role of the card in our lives continues, and its ability to document social change and reflect our outlook means that cards both give pleasure and reveal much about our lives. The 20 years that cover the main period of postcard production (1890–1910) is something of a golden era, and many of the cards printed then are expensive today. For those with restricted budgets there are, however, plenty of postcards to be collected and enjoyed from other periods.

On this page the postcards shown are (*top left*) Brighton, Sussex, "Night View", "hold to the light" card by Frederick Hartmann (*see page 17*), **£8–10/$13–16**; (*below left*) a rare panoramic postcard by Valentine & Sons Ltd of the 1908 Franco-British Exhibition, London, **£12–15/$20–24**; and (*above*) "Quite all (W)Right", 1910, a Woolstone Brothers (Milton Series) folding cut out novelty card, **£15–18/$24–30**.

Condition and pricing of cards

Generally accepted standard gradings are MINT condition (as if straight from the printer); NEAR MINT (slight discoloration due to ageing); EXCELLENT (almost mint with no faults: it may be postally used or unused, with writing only on the address side; clean, fresh-looking image); VERY GOOD (slightly rounded or blunted corners, may have faint creases that do not detract from the overall appearance, postally used or unused, but with no obvious fading); GOOD (corners are rounded with noticeable, slight bending or creases, postally used or unused, with possibly some fading on the address side); FAIR (soiling, fading, creases, damage, writing or postmarks affecting the picture side. Buy these cards only if they are rare or to act as placeholders in a series collection.).

Early cards

The earliest postcards were produced in Austria in 1870, originally as an inexpensive form of communication. They were made of thin, buff-coloured card, with an imprinted stamp, and space for the address on the front, and correspondence on the reverse. Postcards soon became more pictorial, with images appearing on the reverse, leaving little space for a message (these cards are known as "undivided back" cards), but in 1902 British publisher Frederick Hartmann introduced the "divided back" format we know today. By the turn of the century, postcards were seen by many as an art form, and were collected for their own sake.

"Grüss aus Salzburg", postally used, postmarked 22 August 1897, c.£12–14/ $20–22

▲ **Austrian souvenir**
Austria was one of the leading developers of the postcard format. In this example, "Correspondenz-karte" is printed on its undivided back, and the views on the front have a vignetted space for a message, here written in pencil. This was fairly typical. Printer's details are given vertically on the left side: "C. Jurischek Kunstverlag, Salzburg, no. 57". This indicates an Austrian printer with at least 56 other cards.

▼ **"Grüss aus" cards**
Souvenir, or "Grüss aus" ("Greetings from"), cards were the first to exploit the pictorial possibilities of the postcard format. In the example below, the undivided address side is printed "PostKarte". There is a pencilled address, but the card is in good condition, with no postal damage. The chromolithoed illustrations are initialled CG, and the unknown printer has monogrammed the card "GH" lower left, with the number 385.

"Grüss aus Biebrich", postally unused, 1897, **£11–12/ $18–20**

"A Park Steed", postally used, dated 1901, **£30–35/$50–55**

FACT FILE

Naming the game
"Postcard collector" is the title most people who collect postcards prefer, but sometimes the title "cartologist" is used. In the USA, another term, "deltiologist", can be applied. Some collectors are more interested in stamps, postmarks, and the postal history aspects of collecting than in the image.

▲ Animal card

This postcard, painted by the popular British military artist Harry Payne, was designed and published by Raphael Tuck, and chromolithoed in Germany. Tuck, already famous for its excellent greetings cards, was active in campaigning against restrictive postal regulations. This card has an undivided back and is number 546 in the "Animal Life" series. Such cards were numbered separately and published in sets of 6 or 12. This is a desirable, artist-signed card, although the writing could detract slightly from the value.

▼ Japanese card

Until 1868, Japan had remained closed to outsiders, yet in 50 years it had become industrialized. At this time, Japan was called the "England of the East", and in 1902 a 20-year alliance with Britain was signed. The front of the card below bears a hand-tinted photolitho illustration; the printer and publisher are anonymous. This card demonstrates the global impact of the approved postcard format.

Japanese, Yokohama, postally used, postmarked 10 April 1902, **£6–7/$9–11**

Korean card, postally used, 1902, **£10–12/$16–20**

▲ Korean card

The card above was sent from Korea, via China, to England, and it has three separate frankings. It is a typical example of an undivided back card with border. The photolithoed illustration (not shown) depicts a Korean lady being carried in a sedan chair, and workers in fields. Cards and pictures from such "exotic" places, when even mainland Europe seemed inaccessible, had an awakening effect on a semi-literate public. A card such as this would certainly have enriched any postcard album.

"London Life, Hyde Park Corner",
postally used, dated 1902,
£8–9/$13–14

▲ Scene from London

This lively drawing of a
woman driving a motor
vehicle alongside a horse-
drawn cart was possibly drawn
by the artist A.K. Macdonald.
It was published by Raphael
Tuck & Sons in its "Art View"
series 612, V, which was
designed in England and
chromolithoed in Saxony.
The Royal warrant and the
Tuck logo of an artist's easel
are just visible behind the
stamp, and it has an
undivided back. This
is an elegant card in
good condition.

▼ European cards

Many cards were printed in
several European languages.
The postcard below is a
typical early 20thC German
card, but it is a French edition
with "Carte Postale" on the
undivided reverse. The
chromolithoed illustration
is beautifully embossed with
"series 041 no. 2142" printed
top left. Its quality and
appearance resemble some of
Tuck's cards printed in Saxony.
The stamped, franked front
reduces the value slightly.

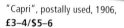

"Capri", postally used, 1906,
£3–4/$5–6

▲ Romantic landscape

This chromolithoed illustration
is part of the excellent
"World's Galleries" series,
printed by the German
company Stengel & Co for
the publisher Misch & Co. The
printer's mark, "Stengel & Co
Dresden", appears on the
front, and the back is printed
similarly to the "Dog and
Frog" card (see left). Records
show that Stengel & Co
printed 30 million cards per
year during the postcard craze.
This card's condition is
considered only fair, since
it is damaged and the stamp
has been removed.

"Dog and Frog", postally used,
1902, **£7–10/$11–16**

▼ Masterworks

Many
publishers
produced
high-quality
reproductions
of the works of great artists.
These postcards were
immensely popular, and avidly
collected, since they pre-dated
"coffee table" art books. This
chromolitho of a Landseer
painting was published by
Misch & Co as one of "The
Great Masters" series number
376. The print quality is
outstanding, and difficult to
match even with modern
techniques. The back is divided.

"Shoeing the Bay Mare",
postally unused, 1906,
£1.50–2/$2.50–3

A "Pyrenese" shepherd, postally
unused, 1906, **£1.50–2/$2.50–3**

▲ Pastoral scene

Good art reproduction was
not readily available at the
beginning of the 20thC, so
postcards were a popular way
of collecting the works of
great artists. Today, however,
the subjects are not always to
modern tastes, so these high-
quality cards are often available
at modest prices. This card,
divided on the back and
number 1129 in the "World's
Galleries" series, was painted
by Rosa Bonheur and printed
by Stendal for Misch & Co.
The quality is good, with
some fading on the reverse.

Postally used cards

While some collectors
prefer unused cards,
most buy both. A
stamp and postmark
establish when a card
was sent and confirm
its authenticity. A
message can add to
the value, perhaps
adding information
about the image. The
correspondent might
be well known or the
stamp rare.

▼ Court cards

The British Postal Authority
dictated the format of
early cards, but in 1895 it
authorized a small card known
as the "court card", 122 x
75mm/5 x 3in. The format
was unpopular, so in 1899 it
permitted the larger Continental
size, 140 x 90mm/5½ x 3½in.
Old stock was used for several
years afterwards as this card,
printed by André and Sleigh
Ltd, demonstrates.

"Holy Trinity Church, Stratford",
postally used, 1907,
£12–15/$20–24

Greetings cards

Before the invention of the postcard in 1869, Christmas and Valentine cards were the only commercial cards available. They were beautiful, and expensively produced, and were occasionally scented. Recognizing the marketing potential, around the turn of the century the postcard industry introduced a wide range of greetings cards for other celebrations, such as birthdays, Easter, New Year's Day, and Thanksgiving and Hallowe'en in the USA, as well as festivals of non-Christian faiths. Souvenir cards also increased greatly in popularity. Greetings postcards were often gilded or embossed, and covered with glitter. They appealed instantly to the public as they were attractive, affordable, and tremendously varied.

▼ **Art Nouveau style**
This postcard, with a divided back, and printed in Germany, combines several period elements. The magic lantern is framed in Art Nouveau style, and covered in forget-me-nots; the four-leaved clovers, or shamrocks, were also typical of the art of this era, as was the glittery text. The card is in excellent condition.

"Greetings from Battersea", postally unused, 1905, **£8–10/$13–16**

Seated female in Tyrolean costume, postally used, 1905, **£4–5/$6–8**

◄ **Christmas cards**
In the early 20thC, people were less sensitive than today about the suitability of a wide range of subjects at Christmas. This card, which was almost certainly printed in Germany, was sent as a Christmas card in 1905. It is chromolithoed and embossed, with silks applied, which makes it an interesting novelty. It has an undivided back, and is in good condition, with corner crease damage only.

"A Happy Christmas",
postmarked 25 December 1912,
£18–22/$30–35

Notable publishers
Raphael Tuck & Sons'
famous trademark of
easel and palette and
the monogram RT&S
date from 1881. The
Royal Warrant was
awarded in 1893. By
1904 the company
had published 15,000
designs.

FACT FILE

▲ Santa theme

The Santa Claus theme is very popular in the US and German postcard markets today. At the time of this card, Santa's outfit was also depicted in brown or blue, as well as the more popular red. This card, printed in Germany, is a two-layered sandwich, with Santa's head moving on a strip fixed between the layers. It is a good-quality, imaginative example of a Christmas card of the time. It has a divided back, and is in excellent condition.

▼ Appliqué cards

In the early 20thC, cards were still produced that were reminiscent of the greetings cards of the mid-19thC – they were made by assembling scraps. This card, which has a divided back and deckled edge, is composed of cut-out, glued-on paper scraps, glitter, and ribbon. Somehow the card survived the post; indeed, the quality is excellent.

"Bonne Année", postally used, 1912, **£8–10/$13–16**

"Easter Greetings", postally
unused, c.1905, **£4–6/$6–9**

▲ Easter cards

Printed in Saxony for Raphael Tuck & Sons' Easter Postcard series, number 3565, this divided-back card bears a written dedication, along with the Royal Warrant, and two Tuck "Easel" logos. Another logo in silver on the front of the card is chromolithoed, embossed, and in a silver frame. The excellent quality of this print makes it a card worth collecting.

"Best Birthday Wishes", postally used, 1908, **£5–8/$8–13**

▼ Birthday cards

This romantic fantasy, featuring a child and bluebirds, was chromolithoed in Germany for the US market. Fabric was applied to the surface, then the whole image was embossed. It has a divided back and is somewhat faded, with postal damage. In general, it is not advisable to buy damaged cards unless they are very scarce examples, or are to act as placeholders for your collection; the US market rejects damaged cards outright.

"Birthday Greetings", postally used, 1906, **£5–6/$8–9**

▲ Hearts and flowers

This busy, colourful design, picturing flowers decorating an early automobile, was chromolithoed by an unknown German printer, with the trademark AMB in a lozenge. It has a divided back, and is embossed, overprinted in gold, then varnished on the front. Similar cards are reproduced for today's trade, so always check cards to ensure that they are not modern reproductions. This card is in excellent condition, with tiny imperfections on two of the corners.

▼ Valentine message

Real hair, feathers, and fabric adorn the surface of this chromolithoed Valentine card. It has a divided back, and "Printed in Germany" on the stamp space. The surface of such cards is extremely delicate, so probably very few were posted without envelopes. Cards such as this are almost 100 years old, and some have aged badly; as a result, they have a historical or novelty value only.

"To My Valentine", postally unused, c.1909, **£12–15/ $20–24** (real hair makes this card more valuable)

"Etoile d'Amour",
postally used, 1913,
£5–6/$8–9

Looking after cards

Keep simple cards in clear wallets as old cards absorb skin oil. Use a soft "putty" rubber to clean off dust marks. Look for albums with acid-free, clear pockets. These don't distort the cards, and they protect their edges, allowing the backs of cards to be seen easily.

▲ Mystery Valentine

This delicate card, like others made of scraps, would have required considerable hand labour to produce. It has elaborately cut edges, applied silver and gold embossed stars, and multi-coloured ribbons. The only printed elements are the text and decoration in Art Nouveau style. It was produced and trade-marked in France, with a divided back, but the printer is anonymous. This example is in very good condition, but spoiled by the stamp applied to the front.

▼ American greeting

By the early 20thC, there was a postcard for every celebration. These types of card are fun for a modest collection. This Thanksgiving card, with a divided back, and "Printed in Germany" on it, was produced for the US market. The design is traditional 19thC. The production quality of this card is excellent – it is chromolithoed and embossed, with gold overprinting.

"Thanksgiving Day", postally unused, c.1909, **£4–6/ $6–9**

▼ Jewish New Year

This chromolithoed image in Art Nouveau style depicts a vignetted picture of a child with giant flowers. It has a divided back, although the greetings are printed in the bottom right corner, suggesting that the design was made for the older, undivided-back cards. Overprinting the image area is the greeting in Hebrew. Most cards at this time were overprinted for minority groups or alternative purposes. The overall condition is good, although it is slightly faded.

"Jewish New Year", postally used, c.1905, **£8–10/ $13–16**

Novelty & speciality cards

Many examples of unusual and speciality cards exist. Sets of cards showing embossed stamps and coins have always been popular. Other sets, sold in threes, sixes, or twelves, made up larger pictures when combined. Some postcards had felt, silk, real hair, and feathers attached to them; others came in diamond and circular forms. The "Write Away" card was a great favourite for those unused to corresponding – an illustrated script was provided for the writer to add a punch line.

The most successful card design had two thin layers sandwiching a variety of elements. These included squeaking cards, rolling-glass-eye cards, hold-to-the-light-cards, and simple concertina "view cards". Comparatively few novelty cards survive today.

▼ **Novelty details**
This "stamp card" is an example of embossed chromolithography, and was printed in Bavaria by Ottmar Zieher, Munich. It has an undivided back, with "Brev-Kort" across the top centre. Stamp cards were made for many of the nations in the Postal Union; they still make an ideal subject for collectors, combining cartology with philately. Several printers came up with similar cards.

"Stamp Card", postally used, 1905, **£8–10/ $13–16**

▶ **Diamond shape**
Probably German, this diamond-shaped card is an example of tinted photolithography. It has an undivided back, printed "Drucksache" (printed matter); this is also stated in other languages. Many postcard formats were tried, and, although postal authorities were more relaxed by 1904, this card had probably been around for some years before it was risked in the British postal system! Even panoramic cards were allowed, provided that there was only a signature.

Diamond-shaped card, postally used, 1904, **£2.50–3/ $4–5**

"Owing to unavoidable circumstances", postally used, postmarked 24 December 1906, **£4.50–6/$7–9**

▼ **Spring mounted**
The undivided back is printed with "Carte postale", which also appears in other languages. The German printer's mark P/F, and "Serie 1882 Gruppe 7", also appear on the back. The card is chromolithoed, and the flower painting is signed by Christina Klein, a known German floral artist. Such cards are popular in the US market, but the hovering butterfly, attached by a spring, is uncommon.

"Butterfly on a spring", postally used, 1905, **£10–12/$16–20** (**£3–4/$5–6** for a basic Klein card)

▲ **"Write Away" cards**
This undivided-back card, produced by Davidson Bros Pictorial Post Cards, "Comic" Series, has a chromolithoed illustration, and a "handwritten" message on the front. The idea was to start off the reluctant correspondent; the illustration would then inspire a comment that was filled in between the lines. These jolly cards proved very popular. This particular one also served as a Christmas card.

▼ **Transparent cards**
Produced in 1906 by Frederick Hartmann, this "Hold to the light" card was number 1 in his transparency series, and was chromolithoed in Berlin. The card's second layer has a varying density that appears only when the card is held to the light (see page 6). Hartmann was a respected publisher and active in persuading the British Post Office to accept the divided-back postcard.

"Royal Pavilion, Brighton", postally used, 1906, **£8–10/$13–16**

▼ Useful cards

Produced by Boots Cash Chemists for its National Coinage Series, the card below was probably printed in Germany. The image of coins is chromolithoed, overprinted with silver and bronze inks, and then embossed. It is a really good piece of printing, and the card is still clean and sharp. This card was useful, as well as beautiful, with its conversion chart for various currencies. Another similar series published by Menker & Huber of Zurich is also desirable.

"Coin card", postally used, 1907, **£8–10/$13–16**

"Chin Chin Chinaman", postally used, 1907, **£12–15/$20–24**

▲ Match-striking card

The divided back of this card, printed in England by Delittle Fenwick & Co, York, has the Defco logo and series number 1189 printed on it. This English printer/publisher specialized in novelty cards, and had its own colour process called Defco-Chrome. Around 1905 the company employed Yoshio Markino, the only known Japanese artist then living in Britain. As well as this card, he also probably worked on a series called "Japru" war-puzzle games.

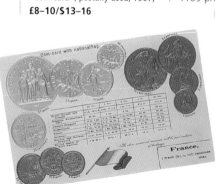

▼ Kaleidoscope cards

Produced by Alfred Stiebel & Co as number 466 in its Alpha series, this divided-back card, printed with "Processed in Prussia", has not been posted, but has a written message dating it. The picture is based on a famous dancer of the period, Loïe Fuller, who swirled her robe up and around her body as she moved. The front of the card is perforated, and an internal disc pivots on a spindle. This card is part of a set of six kaleidoscopes. Loïe Fuller also inspired Art Nouveau bronzes and table lamps.

"Kaleidoscope", postally unused, 1911, **£30–35/$50–55**

"L'amour de Pierrot", postally unused, 1912, **£12–15/$20–24**

▲ Fantasy cards

Alfred Stiebel & Co changed its name to the Alphalsa Publishing Co in 1912. Such changes help collectors to date cards; this one is unused, with a divided back labelled "The Alpha Postcard". Fantasy cards are still popular among collectors in Europe. The secondary images make up the dominant image, which in this case is the skull. There are also several erotic cards in this style, and many of famous people such as Wagner. Such cards make an intriguing collection.

▼ Noisy cards

Max Ettlinger & Co produced many squeaking cards for the children's market, often bearing nursery rhymes. When the mechanism in the card is squeezed, air escapes out of a hole in the address side so that the card "squeaks". This card has a divided back, with no publisher or printer credited. It is a colour photolitho print, probably British, and in excellent condition. The address side is somewhat faded, but the card still has a good, clear squeak!

"We're longing to hear ...", postally unused, c.1914, **£9–12/$14–20**

Alpha

In 1910 this was the tradename of fine art publisher Alfred Stiebel & Co, London. Although not a major publisher, this company produced varied and high-quality postcards of many subjects, from novelty cards with moving parts, to silk cards woven in England or France.

▼ Moving parts

This divided-back card bears the sole agent's name, J. Picot, Paris, so presumably the card was made in France, and sent somehow during World War I. The hat rocks on a pivot to reveal two views (see page 5). The message speaks of the difficulties of getting suitably silly cards at the time, which says much about those sad days when the postcard mania came to an abrupt end.

"She loves me – she loves me not", postally unused, 1916, **£5–7/$8–11**

Humour

Newspapers and satirical publications, such as *Punch*, were training grounds for many well-known comic artists in the early 1900s – Tom Browne, Lance Thackeray, and Phil May, for example. The postcard craze provided a great deal of employment for these and other artists whose work is comparatively undocumented but worth collecting. The humour of that time can seem crude or even offensive today, but the situations shown in the best cards are as amusing and fresh now as they were then. There is a wealth of material in topical gags dealing with the then novelties, such as the telephone and wireless, and sports such as bicycling.

"Spooning by moonlight", postally used, 1908, **£4–6/$6–9**

▶ **"Tom B"**
Produced by Davidson Bros, this divided-back card was printed in England and signed by Tom Browne (1872–1910), a popular and prolific artist. "Tom B", who trained in lithography with a Nottingham printer, became a very successful magazine illustrator in Europe and the USA. Most of his output was through Davidson Bros, and he even commissioned other artists for the company. His subjects have a universal appeal, and his style is still fresh today.

▼ **"Low" humour**
This humorous, divided back card was issued by Inter-Art Co, Comique series number 5926, and signed by Donald McGill (1875–1962). Probably printed in Britain, this was a long-running series of cards and helped bring McGill to prominence. His brash, low humour may have offended some people, but such cards have an evergreen popular appeal. The cards varied in quality, and between the two World Wars they were considered vulgar. Nevertheless, many survived, and are now seen as simple fun.

"Oh, Cyril", postally unused, c.1912, **£4–6/$6–9**

DO I FEEL SHY?
LIFT MY PATCH UP, GIRLS, AND SEE!

"Do I feel shy?", postally unused, 1911, **£9–12/$14–20**

▲ Comic series
This divided-back card, number 10 in Bamforth & Co's Joke Card series, was photolithoed in England. The artist is unknown, but his initials, "HY", are on the front, bottom right. This cheeky fellow is part of Bamforth's century-long tradition of making the public laugh. The good-natured caricature would also be of interest to collectors of "Black history". Bamforth had an enormous output of comic cards by well-known artists, such as Douglas Tempest and Arnold Taylor.

▼ Valentine
Valentine & Sons Ltd, Dundee, has been a prolific producer of cards since the "court card" days. It claims to have been the first British publisher to have produced cards with the picture completely covering the front. The company won numerous prizes for its cards at exhibitions at the turn of the century. An unusual Valentine panorama card is shown on page 6. The artist card below is by Lawson Wood (1878–1957), and is number 3941 in the "Lawson Wood" postcard series.

"Grandpop's bid for the Atlantic Blue Ribbon", postally used, 1938, **£5–6/$8–9**

Valentine & Sons Ltd
Early Valentine "court cards" have initials on the reverse – "V&S,D" or "V&S Series". In 1902, it was the first publisher to produce cards with the picture covering one side and a divided back. The company's logo was used around 1909. Valentine continued production until 1968.

▼ Charming humour
Mabel Lucie Attwell (1879–1962) was another Valentine artist. Her earliest cards date from 1911, and she simultaneously illustrated and wrote books for children, while producing sets for Valentine until World War II. Her distinctive style and charming, humorous characters were continually reprinted and retain their popularity to this day.

"Two happy ladies", postally unused, c.1935, **£6–8/$9–13**

Entertainment

Entertainers loved the postcard because it was the ideal form of publicity for variety halls or opera houses. The immense public interest in collecting cards meant that every new issue was eagerly awaited, and the advertisements they carried were thus widely distributed. Alphonse Mucha, the Art Nouveau artist, came to wide public notice through his commissions to produce postcards for the actress Sarah Bernhardt. Performers started to have studio portraits made, which were then printed as postcards and distributed. These were sometimes signed at "sessions", much as books are today. There were many such autographed cards, and they are widely collected. As working people began to enjoy more leisure, their parties and pageants were frequently recorded as postcards.

▼ Music-hall troupe

This hand-tinted photograph bears the photographer's name, "Sazerac, Paris", on the front, bottom left; "Marque deposée G. Piprot, Paris" and "Serie no.857–Th.108" on the address side. The *artistes* depicted seem to have either a stage-set background or the photographer's studio, but obviously it's a troupe from a music hall. This wonderful, lively, French-produced card was postally used in England and is in excellent condition.

"Showgirls", postally used, 1906, **£3–4/$5–6**

▼ Theatre cards

This real photographic card, produced by "Rotary Photographic Series", photographers Foulsham & Banfield, shows two artists, Miss Gertie Millar (Mitzi) and Mr Edmund Payne (Max Moddelkopf), from *The Girls from Gothenburg*. Gertie Millar was a great stage artist and very popular. She began her career as a "Gaiety Girl", and had numerous big hits, including this show. Edmund Payne was a popular comedian at the Gaiety Theatre, London.

"The Girls from Gothenburg", postally used, 1907, **£1.50–2/$2.50–3**

▼ Play promotion

Postcards such as the one below were usually circulated when theatre attendance started to fall. Neither the designer nor the printer of this card is credited, but it is photolithographically printed. It is a divided-back card depicting a play by Maurice Maeterlinck. The fantasy story of fairies, with actors in animal costumes, had a *Peter Pan* atmosphere and Isadora Duncan-style dancing. Shown at the Haymarket Theatre, London, the play was successful, running for 276 performances.

"The Blue Bird for Happiness*"*, postally unused, c.1910, **£14–15/$22–24**

▼ Musical entertainment

The rear of this card reads "P. Michael Faraday presents", with the performances and the times. The "musical entertainment" started in 1912 at the Lyric Theatre, London, and ran for 385 performances. The card's striking illustration is by "L" Barribal, better known for his paintings of glamorous women. Although this card is in very good condition, there is damage to a corner.

"The Girl in the Taxi", postally used, 1913, **£14–15/$22–24**

Bamforth

In 1902, Bamforth used studio sets and live models to create sets of postcards of popular songs and hymns. He produced 24 new songs twice a year from 1903 to 1910. During World War I, over 250 songs, propaganda, and sentimental cards were produced. Bamforth cards are still popular.

▼ "Pierrot Group"

Pierrot is based on one of the Commedia dell'Arte characters, who has wild swings of mood; it was a fashionable image in tune with the times. Fancy dress was also all the rage, and Pierrot or Pierrette costumes were very popular. Art Deco style made extensive use of Pierrot images and costumed period figures. This postcard possibly depicts an end-of-pier concert party troupe. Using real photography, the card is in very good condition and has "Tiddy, Folkestone" embossed in the bottom left corner.

Pierrot group, postally unused, c.1925, **£7–9/$11–14**

Glamour

Glamour cards both idolized women and depicted them as erotically charged objects. While the Anglo-Saxons generally portrayed the refined and corseted lady, the French showed Eve as the temptress in all her physicality. Because of the notoriety of such nude cards, the French authorities attempted to make models wear body stockings in the late 19thC, and photographs were often retouched. They were hidden for decades, but we can now enjoy the sauciness of such boudoir cards – popular as this genre was, these postcards were not destined to appear in a family postcard album or to be in the post! World War I encouraged the flowering of the pin-up, and many such cards had a patriotic flavour.

"Nude",
postally unused,
c.1904, body
stocking
£8–10/
$13–16, true
nude **£12–14/**
$20–22

◀ Calling men!

It has been suggested that women had a virtual monopoly on collecting cards in the late 19thC, and that cards such as this were used to encourage men to collect them! The notoriety of these cards contributed to the "naughty" image which Paris acquired at the turn of the century.

This is the archetypal "French Postcard". It is a real photograph produced by Stebbing, Paris, with "H de Serville" printed across the front.

▼ Respectable glamour

This card represents the Anglo-Saxon counterblast to the "French Postcard"; here the model is well buttoned-up and respectable. The postcard image was painted by Philip Boileau (1864–1917), who was born in Canada and died in New York. Well-known as a glamour artist, he was published mainly by Reinthal & Newman in the USA. His work is still very collectable.

This card was published by Wildt & Kray, London, and printed in the USA.

"Tomorrow",
postally
unused,
c.1907,
£8–10/
$13–16

Waitress with Parisienne Easter eggs, postally unused, c.1914, **£8–10/$13–16**

▲ **Pin-ups**
Here is patriotic sauciness for soldiers during World War I – a wonderful, fresh, and funny image, which was just right as a pin-up in the trenches. The card, signed by Leon Peltier, is in the "Editions Delta", Paris, series number 22–110, with Trichromatic printing (three colours plus black), and was printed in France. Leon Peltier was a French painter who specialized in *deshabillé* pictures, which were invariably light-hearted and amusing. The pin-ups of this period make a fascinating collection.

"British Destroyer", postally unused, c.1914, **£14–16/$22–26**

▲ **William "L" Barribal**
This is a divided-back card by Inter-Art Co in its "Artistique" series number 1588, photolithoed in Britain, signed by the British artist "L" Barribal. Barribal was a versatile artist, with much graphic poster work and wonderful paintings of alluring women and girls to his credit. He is an undervalued artist who painted numerous wartime pin-ups, and there are a number of his postcard paintings available today.

"Les Obus Pacifiques", postally unused, c.1914, **£15–16/$24–26**

▲ **Sager pin-ups**
Artist-signed by Xavier Sager, this divided-back card was produced by French publisher Noyaer, in its "Fantaisies Trichromes" series. Small logos advertising stick-on shoe soles are printed around the margin of the address side. It may be an early free-advertising card. The card is part of a good series of Sager pin-ups.

Children & animals

Cards depicting children and animals that stand out, always popular subjects, usually have a very recognisable style. Louis Wain (1860–1939), for example, was an artist fascinated by cats, portraying them with human, somewhat manic, characteristics. Many other artists illustrated dogs, frogs, pigs, ducks, and mice, often dressed in clothes. Children were very popular for marketing products, such as Pears soap and Fry's chocolate. Nursery illustrators, such as Rose O'Neill and Ellen Clapsaddle, were both stylish US artists, and Mabel Lucie Attwell was a popular British artist known for her drawings of chubby children.

▼ **Prodigious cats**
From 1900, Louis Wain produced around 600 drawings a year for many years, mostly of cats. Perhaps because of this enormous output, the public tired of his work. He later entered an asylum and died there in poverty. Today his cards are eagerly sought by collectors and can fetch high prices. This signed card was produced by Charles Voisey.

▲ **Charming cats**
This card has a divided back, and was produced by C.W. Faulkner & Co, series number 193c, designed in England, and printed in Germany. Helena Maguire, who illustrated many Victorian greetings cards, has been suggested as the artist, since much of her work was certainly recycled for postcards. Other series, by Misch & Co and SH & Co, seem to be by the same artist. These are charming cards, and worth collecting.

"An interesting lecture", postally unused, 1904, **£14–15/ $22–24**

"She's awfully pretty", postally unused, c.1903, **£60–65/ $95–105**

▼ Early Valentine & Sons cards

This is an early card from the now famous publisher Valentine & Sons Ltd. Although postally unused, it dates from c.1905 and appears to be lithographically produced. The illustrator of this study is not credited, but the subject matter clearly reflects a more rational attitude to race coexisting alongside popular, but irrational, prejudice. The card has a divided back printed with "Postcard", "Printed in Great Britain", and "Valentine's Series"; there is no logo or number.

"A Study in Black and White", postally unused, c.1905, **£7–8/$11–13**

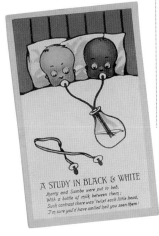

A STUDY IN BLACK & WHITE
*Harry and Sambo were put to bed,
With a bottle of milk between them;
Such contrast there was 'twixt each little head,
I'm sure you'd have smiled had you seen them!*

Present Arms!

"Present Arms", postally unused, c.1910, **£2.50–3/$4–5**

▲ Patriotism

Produced by Misch & Co Ltd for its Real Photo postcards series 3179/1, the subject was photographed in England, and printed in Germany, and has an "Aristophot" trademark on the divided back. The flags and other elements have been tinted or handpainted after printing. The card's message is basically one of patriotism as demonstrated by young children. Such sentiments were encouraged during the pre-war years.

Printing techniques

Letterpress: this uses a relief or raised printing surface, which is inked and pressed onto the print surface. Tones are reproduced by their conversion into dots of differing densities.

Collotype: this is a sharper relief process. From 1900s to 1920s this was the common process used for photographic reproduction.

FACT FILE

"The Balcony Scene", postally used, 1911, **£2.50–3/$4–5**

▲ Puppy appeal

Puppies and kittens have an undeniable appeal, and packaging them in a semi-literary fashion added to a basically soppy picture, something well recognized even in modern advertising techniques! This is a divided-back card by Raphael Tuck & Sons, "Animal Studies" Series number 1352. It bears the usual "Royal Warrant" and "Easel" logos.

Art Nouveau & Art Deco

Around 1900, a new art movement known as Art Nouveau developed. This style was characterized by sensuous, swirling, decorative lines simulating plant forms. Since it broke the constrained forms of the Victorian period, it was labelled "decadent" by its detractors. The style developed during the heyday of the postcard, and artists associated with it gained enormous publicity. The work of such well-known artists in this style is both popular and expensive.

Art Deco arrived in the mid-1920s. The subjects are less sensuous than in the Art Nouveau style, with simplified or streamlined forms. Idealized figures and animals in romantic settings, and transatlantic liners, are typical themes. Although the style is popular, you can still find good cards.

Mucha card, near mint condition, postally unused, c.1900, **£200–250/ $320–400**

▼ Alphonse Mucha

Mucha (1860–1939) is the most famous of the Art Nouveau artists; although a Czech by birth, he worked mostly in France. His work, which is eagerly collected, and therefore valuable, falls into two periods, the earlier of which is the more desirable. Most of Mucha's postcards were adapted from poster designs, and rare examples are highly prized; one such poster recently sold for more than £10,000/ $16,000. The condition of the work is most important.

▼ Raphael Kirchner

Kirchner (1876–1917) was born and trained in Vienna. He moved to Paris around 1900, and to New York in 1914, at the outbreak of World War I. This image was designed for postcards printed by S. Hildesheimer & Co in huge numbers. There is an alternative version without sunrays. Kirchner produced mainly "glamour" pictures and his output was prodigious. Rarer Kirchner cards are in the price range £80–100/ $130–160.

"Sunrays", postally unused, c.1900, **£50–55/ $80–90**

Printing techniques
Lithography: this uses
a flat printing surface
and involves an artist
drawing a design in
oily ink onto a stone
or zinc plate. This design
attracts oily ink; paper
pressed onto the surface
captures a mirror image
of the design.
Chromolithography: the
design is transferred by
a photographic process.
Each colour requires a
separate plate and is
printed separately.

FACT FILE

"Lawn Tennis", postally unused,
c.1900, **£20–25/$32–40**

▼ Romantic escapism

The expression "Art Deco"
came into use after the
Exhibition of Decorative Arts,
Paris, 1925. It combined both
romantic fantasy and "jazz
age" modern imagery. This
beautiful, hand-finished card
in excellent condition is
typical of the genre, with
idealized femininity offset with
fashionable, elegant hunting
dogs. Painted, but not signed,
by G. Mesohini, it is part of
the ARS NOVA Series printed
in Italy.

Crinoline lady with dogs, postally
unused, c.1925, **£20–25/$32–40**

▲ Nouveau/Deco

Meissner & Buch, Leipzig,
was a fine-art printer with
a high reputation for quality
postcards. Painted by Swedish
artist Brynolf Wennerberg
(1866–1950), this beautiful,
chromolithoed card shows,
with its curving outer frame,
Art Nouveau characteristics,
although the style anticipates
the Art Deco periods with its
areas of flat colour and
simplified shapes.

▼ Chiostri

Carlo Chiostri and his
daughter made several series
cards in the 1920s that are
typical of the Art Deco style.
He also produced many
images of children and small
Pierrots. This composition,
published by Ballerine &
Fratini, Italy, is framed within
a diamond shape, and features
several characters from the
Commedia dell'Arte. It is a
very attractive theatrical card
in excellent condition.

Pierrots and Columbine, postally
unused, c.1926, **£30–35/$50–55**

Topographical cards

Most collectors have a few cherished topographical cards in their collections, often featuring scenes of a neighbourhood as much as a century ago. At postcard fairs, topographical cards tend to outnumber all others. The big plate cameras and slow film made street photography at the beginning of the 20thC a cumbersome process. Since photographers frequently took such pictures when it was early or quiet, the shots often lack vitality. However, good photographers knew how to overcome the problems, and their work is exciting, but usually fairly expensive. Artists' views are also popular now, as they were then, particularly if signed.

▼ **Street scene essentials**
This card shows a composition one would hope to find on a good street scene anywhere: pedestrians, a variety of vehicles, advertisements, street furniture, and a station. A country photographer might have had only a few cards printed for sale, so today these would be rare. In the cities, however, many such cards would have been printed. This is a printed card by Charles Martin. A real photographic card with a glossy finish would be more valuable.

Henley Bridge and church, Oxfordshire, postally used, 1908, **£2.50–4/$4–6**

Uxbridge Road Station, Shepherds Bush, London, postally used, 1906, **£10–12/ $14–20**

▲ **Popular landscapes**
This Raphael Tuck & Sons "oilette" card shows a view of Henley by Henry Wimbush, and is typical of many popular, signed landscapes painted around 1900; many of these cards are undervalued, and just as attractive as those of A.R. (Alfred Robert) Quinton, whose cards are sought after, and expensive.

"LL" cards

Louis (sometimes given as Lucien) Lévy's great strength as a photographer was his eye for an interesting subject, which most topographical photographers would probably have ignored. In this picture, the people of the Pas de Calais are shown to have converted upturned boats into homes. Such a sharp photographic record is a telling social document, giving us greater insight into the past than the average shot of village housing. "LL" cards are numerous in the UK and France.

"LL" city scenes

Lévy's sharp, atmospheric postcards of large cities, such as London and Paris, are both easy to find and inexpensive. He also made wonderful, photographic postcards of towns and resorts all over Britain and France, but, because fewer were printed, these are now rarer. This tinted card shows Trafalgar Square underground station under construction.

"87 London, entrance to Strand ..." Trafalgar Square, London, postally used, 1910, £7–8/$11–13

Oilettes

First produced in 1903, Tuck's famous "oilettes" series was described as "veritable miniature oil paintings" and was of very high quality. A wide range of sets was produced, and many were frequently reprinted. Their value today depends on the artist, the subject, and the rarity value.

City monuments

Built in 1906, the Singer Building was, briefly, the world's tallest building. Designed by Ernest Flagg for the Singer Sewing Machine Company, the building stood in a densely populated, urban area. The land values subsequently soared, and New York changed from a harbour of low-rise buildings to a high-rise metropolis. The card below was published by the Success Postal Card Co, New York.

Environs de Boulogne-Equihen, postally used, 1908, £5–7/$8–11

Singer Building, New York, postally used, 1913, £1.50–2/ $2.50–3

Transport

Shipping was at its peak just before World War I. Ocean liners, such as the *Titanic*, were the stars, but postcards also featured battleships, paddle steamers, and a huge variety of craft. Postal agreements allowed ships to frank postage stamps en route. Similarly, franking was carried out on mail trains in Europe, and postmarks and machine cancellations are very popular with collectors. Railway companies were growing, and advertised widely – thousands of cards were printed showing engines, royal trains, stations, maps, and hotels. After the famous Wright Brothers' flight in 1905, aerial events were celebrated with special postal cancellations, and in Britain the Air Post was inaugurated for the coronation of George V in 1911. Early aerial postings and cards are both eagerly sought and valuable.

P & O official card, postally used, 1903, **£12–15/ $20–24**

▲ **Shipping cards**

In a book such as this there is insufficient space to deal with the complex subject of postmarks, but those made on board ship are some of the most valuable. This undivided-back card was produced by Andrew Boyd & Co of Newcastle on Tyne. It is an early chromolithoed vignette posted from Aden (The Yemen).

▼ **Railway cards**

Although cards such as the one below were issued in sets of 12, this is the only railway set published by J.W. Bland, London. Railway cards were generally printed in huge quantities, and there are still many around. Since the value of such cards is determined by both the line shown and their rarity, it is still possible to make a collection of train cards inexpensively.

"Aberdeen Express", postally used, 1909, **£3–5/ $5–8**

Printing techniques

Photogravure: this is a photo-mechanical method that simulates etching for engraving copper printing-plates. It is the best method for reproducing tonal variation.

Offset: this print quality is similar to that of letterpress. It uses a flat surface and cylindrical plates for rotary printing, using oil-based printing inks.

FACT FILE

"Nordsee–Linie–Hamburg",
postally used, 1903,
£25–30/$40–50

▲ Poster-like cards

This chromolithoed card is what the British postcard collectors of the period were demanding of their publishers. It is a dramatic, poster-like card expounding the delights of steamship trips. Cards made from actual posters of the same period are expensive, while cards with much advertising content are generally even more valuable. The artwork and printing of this card were by Jugens & Bornemann, Hamburg.

▼ Aeroplane cards

On the rear of the card below is a splendid blurb: "A super Handley Page aeroplane fitted with 4 Rolls-Royce engines of 350hp each. It carries 1000 gallons of petrol weighing about 3.5 tons. The wheels on this machine are 5ft high." Early aviation cards are expensive, but those produced when the novelty of the plane had worn off are less so. This card was by the Alphalsa Publishing Co Ltd.

A four-engine Handley Page aeroplane, postally unused, c.1918, **£8–10/$13–16**

Great Eastern motorbus, postally used, 1907, **£15–20/$24–32**

▲ Unofficial cards

Although the card above is an interesting, hand-tinted, photographic card, it is not an official Great Eastern Railway advertising card, and so would not have been printed in large numbers. Motorbuses were novelties in 1907, but by the end of World War I they had taken over from horse-drawn vehicles. This card has a divided back, and was printed and published by F Kehrhahn and Co, Bexley and London.

Reportage

At the end of the 19th and beginning of the 20th centuries, the postcard was important both for communication and as a news medium. As photographic technology improved, with smaller cameras and faster film, more photographers experimented with shooting outside. There was a steady demand for "news" photos for immediate distribution – fire scenes, mine disasters, shipwrecks, and train crashes were all recorded, printed as postcards, and sent by the public. Postcards also recorded national sporting events, parades, and pageants. Holiday-makers would have their portraits taken at the seaside by local photographers, and send them to their friends, as postcards, giving us insight into life in another age.

Funeral procession of Edward VII, postally used, June 1910, **£6–7/$9–11** (normal funeral cards c.**£2/$3**)

▲ **Commemorative cards**
Since newspaper photo reproduction of the time was poor, a photograph as striking as this sold well as a postcard. Such postcards were an ideal medium for recording local and national news events, together with State occasions. Cards were sometimes produced the same day as the event. This divided-back card was photographed by Louis Lévy and printed in collotype.

▲ **Disasters**
This real photograph postcard by F.C. Cooper, Eastbourne, records a local event. The print run would have been limited, so the card is now rare. Shipwrecks and lifeboats were popular postcard themes, as were accidents, and natural disasters of all types. "Rough Seas" was another popular theme, and many photographic cards were produced showing a variety of seaside resorts and harbour walls being pounded by stormy seas!

Stranded SS *Eastfield*, postally used, 1909, **£18–20/$30–32**

▼ Social history

Although much of the text is missing on this real photograph postcard, there is plenty of information to date it exactly. The newspaper placards hold the clues: "Asquith shouted down in the Commons"; the partial address on the card would also help an enthusiast to track down the location of the shop. (This one was in North London.) Such information increases both the interest and the value of a card to collectors. The card below is of particular interest as the shop window shown is clearly full of contemporary postcards, albums, greetings cards, and paper ephemera; there are even large advertisements for Tuck's postcards. A veritable treasure house!

The Montagu Stationery Stores, postally unused, c.1911, **£35–40/$55–65**

▼ London life series

London life was a popular subject for several publishers, and there were similar series produced. This card is an unlisted rarity by a well-known photographer/publisher, Gordon Smith. It is a clear, attractive image of an Italian ice-cream cart with elaborate paintings on the front panels. The card was printed in Germany in collotype, and hand tinted.

Ice-cream cart, postally used, 1920, **£30–35/$50–55** (similar series c.**£15/$24**)

Types of London Life. Ice Cream Stall.

Topical cards

From 1901, "current events" cards were published on a subscription basis. By 1905, public demand for these cards was so great that the "Illustrated Daily Postcard" was published, featuring an item of interest that occurred each day.

▼ News events

Even as late as the mid-1930s, there was still a demand for real photographic postcards of news events, particularly as photographs had replaced illustrations in most magazines and newspapers. As there are many such postcards on the market today, card-buying had perhaps become a habit where local events were concerned, or there may have been a market for souvenir cards of an event of national significance. This tinted card was produced by Valentine & Sons Ltd Postcards.

Souvenir of the Crystal Palace fire, postally unused, 1936, **£8–10/$13–16**

SOUVENIR OF THE CRYSTAL PALACE, DESTROYED BY FIRE, NOV. 30TH 1936.

Exhibitions

The 1889 Paris Exhibition was the first event to exploit the commercial possibilities of postcards. The Eiffel Tower, star of the show, had facilities at its summit for posting cards with specially franked stamps, and this established postcards as souvenirs in France. Many postcard sets were sold at the 1896 Colombian Exhibition in Chicago. And at the 1900 Paris Exposition Universelle, imaginative buildings and pavilions sold cards that publicized the exhibition around the world. Early exhibition cards are eagerly sought by collectors, and these are available and inexpensive today. Cards bearing commemorative postmarks are most sought after.

"Exposition Universelle 1900 – La Porte Monumentale" postally unused, 1900, **£2–4/ $3–6**

▲ **Paris exhibition 1900**
The success of the Exposition Universelle in 1900 helped to unify France. The spectacular entrance depicted was also known as the "Porte Binet" after its architect. Three huge arches were covered by a dome, minarets lit the gateway, and a towering female figure of Paris sat at the summit. The lines of the building were picked out by thousands of light bulbs. Printed in collotype and hand tinted, this near mint-condition card has an undivided back.

▼ **Glasgow exhibition 1901**
This wonderful interpretation by Belgian artist Henri Cassiers (1858–1944) of the Glasgow International Exhibition entrance is a loose Art Nouveau style that gives vitality to what could have been an ordinary view. There are 12 cards in the set of the exhibition by Cassiers: two show the exhibition, while the others are of Glasgow streets and the Clyde shipyards. The set sold for 1 shilling (5p/8c) at the time. A great deal of Cassiers' work was published – as a postcard artist he is much underrated.

"Glasgow International Exhibition 1901", postally unused, 1901, **£12–15/ $20–24**

"Court of the Universe", postally
unused, 1915, **£3–5/$5–8**

▲ Panama-Pacific
International Exhibition
Held in San Francisco in 1915,
this exhibition celebrated the
completion of the Panama
Canal and the 400th
anniversary of the Pacific
Ocean's discovery. It was
also a morale-builder after
the devastating effects of
the 1906 earthquake. The
tallest building in the
exhibition was a 43-storey
"Tower of Jewels", so-named
because of the many
thousands of coloured
and light-reflecting glass
"jewels" that hung from it,
shimmering as sea-breezes
moved them. This
exhibition card was
published by Chas Weidner,
787 Market Street,
San Francisco.

"The German Pavilion", postally
unused, 1937, **£4–5/$6–8**

▼ Paris exhibition 1937
Although there were probably
many cards printed for this
exhibition, few are seen at
postcard fairs today. The
pavilion depicted below was
designed by Albert Speer in
his usual, heavy, monumental
style, and was an excellent
example of Third Reich
architecture, seen on this real
photographic card in its pre-
World War II context. This
card was published in France
by H. Chipault, Boulogne.

"The Trylon and the Perisphere",
postally unused, 1939, **£2–3/$3–5**

▲ New York World's Fair
After the Depression,
Americans looked forward
to a future that was simple,
orderly, and rational. This
utopian vision was realized
by the World's Fair architects,
who designed pavilions that
still look modern today. This
artist's impression depicts a
futuristic world. The card was
printed by Tichnor Brothers
Inc., New York.

Advertising

Having already established a practice of giving away luxurious trade cards to customers, advertisers even copied the first issue of British postcards in 1870 to exploit them for advertising purposes. Postcards were inexpensive to send to existing or potential customers, and the enthusiasm for cards at the time meant that the customer was likely to keep them, so the cards would serve as subtle reminders. Cards were frequently designed to appeal to children, showing pretty, nursery-rhyme images, which guaranteed that they would be placed in albums and shown to loving relatives. Children, puppies, and kittens were common subjects, as were royalty and patriotic images to suggest reliability or honesty. Many well-known brand names were established in this period as a result, to some degree, of the effectiveness of postcard advertising.

▼ **Advertising souvenir**
Produced as a souvenir for the Franco-British Exhibition 1908, this striking poster-like card is signed by the French artist Eugène Ogé. Ogé also produced cards for Tuck's London series "Les Affiches célèbres". Valentine & Sons were the official suppliers of postcards at this exhibition, and their cards are both still available and cheap. Those postmarked at the White City and stamped Franco-British Exhibition are of particular interest. Many exhibitors produced their own advertising cards. Again, cards that are specially stamped have greater interest.

"Guyot Braces", postally unused, 1908, **£20–25/$32–40**

Lipton tea factory, postally used, 1908, **£3–5/ $5–8**

◄ **Tea cards**
Lipton produced a series of six cards, all of which show its tea plantations in Ceylon (Sri Lanka), and its name appears on the roof of the building featured. Another series, by the publisher Faulkner, shows plantation workers plucking the leaves. Such cards helped strengthen the public image of Lipton against fierce competition. This one was published by the Photochrom Co. Ltd, London and Detroit. Cards advertising food are quite numerous and inexpensive.

▼ Chinatown

The card below features a famous Oriental bazaar that stood at the corner of California Street and Grant Avenue, San Francisco. Later versions depict different flags, pedestrians, and vehicles, but this exotic representation of Chinatown has travelled around the world advertising itself. The card has a dragon trademark, and the design elements on the reverse are all in Art Nouveau style. The immense variety of advertising cards available makes this one of the most varied and inexpensive themes to collect.

"Sing Fat Co Inc", postally unused, *c.*1915, **£4–6/$6–9**

"Standard Bread Series", postally used, *c.*1911, **£10–12/$16–20**

▲ Advertising "artworks"

This unusual, "art textured" card, with its bold and humorous illustration of a small boy, was expensive to produce. The illustration was lithographed onto beige, textured card by an unknown artist, "O". It has much in common with "A Study in Black and White" (see *page 27*) by the same publisher (Valentine & Sons). The quality of illustration, and the print, on cards of this period were exceptional, yet these "artworks" are still inexpensive to buy today.

SING FAT CO., INC.
CHINESE AND JAPANESE BAZAAR
S. W. COR. CALIFORNIA AND DUPONT STS.
CHINATOWN, SAN FRANCISCO CAL.
美國金正埠生發公司

(see *page 27*)

▼ Royal approval

Royalty was used to endorse products in the early 1900s, and a number of such ads appear on postcards. Edward VII and Queen Alexandra featured on a picture of the British Fleet advertising Gossage's Soap, "The Right Sort", and Edward VII was shown with a cup of Horniman's tea, "A Right Royal Drink".

FACT FILE

▼ Whisky cards

Produced by Raphael Tuck and Sons, this card is an "oilette" by artist Harry Payne (1858–1927), and is based on a previous black-and-white card called "Empire". The composition has been repainted and updated for this whisky manufacturer. Many of Payne's cards and cut-outs were similarly adapted. His main themes were military topics and rural landscapes. All his work is popular, and has risen sharply in price.

"Claymore, Old Parr and Sandy Macdonald", postally unused, 1924, **£25–30/ $40–50**

Early political cards

Cards from the early part of the 20thC offer fascinating insights into historical events, showing us clearly the issues that vexed the public at the time. In Britain the movement for women's suffrage is such a topic, and makes a perfect study for collectors, with a wealth of good material available. Further themes that have generated interesting cards in the past are the development of the trade unions, Irish politics, protectionism versus free trade with regard to Britain before World War I, and conscientious objection before World War I. Subjects such as the relations between servants and mistresses, changing social customs and expectations, and "hard times" were also all continuing common themes for postcards.

"When women vote", postally used, 1907, **£20–25/ $32–40**

▲ Women's suffrage
Universal suffrage was often treated as a joke in the early 1900s: public reaction to women who dared to express opinions publicly, and demanded the right to vote, was generally less than sympathetic. Although postcards with women's suffrage as a theme make a wonderful collection, the topic is popular, and cards are not cheap. This one was published by Mitchell & Watkins.

▼ Direct action
This card is signed by the artist, but the signature is unknown, and it lacks print/publisher information. Direct action to secure suffrage for women in Britain sometimes, as suggested below, involved the hounding of unsympathetic politicians – in this case Prime Minister Asquith. More militant protesters chained themselves to railings in public places, smashed windows, and interrupted public meetings. Cards illustrating personalities or accidents can cost £40–120/ $65–190 today.

"Chase me; Votes for Women", postally unused, 1910, **£15–18/ $24–30**

"Killing the British Lion", postally used, 1910, **£4–6/$6–9**

▲ Empire trade
At this period the UK relied on trade with countries in the British Empire; these countries were, in turn, a captive market for UK goods. Countries outside the system viewed it as unfair, and they would attempt to gain entry into the UK's protected market. This political card was published by the Conservative and Constitutional Association, Westminster, London.

▼ Irish rebellion
The history of the Irish struggle for independence is a long one, and this card commemorates a particularly tragic incident which took place at Easter 1916. The Sinn Fein movement had organized the Easter Rising, and subsequently declared a republic. When it failed to receive the support it had expected, the movement was harshly suppressed by the British Army after bloody fighting in the streets of Dublin. Fourteen of the uprising's leaders were executed, and, after a controversial trial, Roger Casement, a leading figure who had been in Germany organizing support for independence, was convicted of treason, and executed. This card represents a form of news reporting, albeit with overtones of propaganda.

"Soldiers holding a Dublin Street", postally unused, 1916, **£14–15/$22–24**

Propaganda?
Photographs of demonstrations in 1905 against Tsarist rule in St Petersburg, Russia, were smuggled out, and made into cards in England. These cards had a ready market with refugees in the East End of London.

"The Great Strike", postally used, 1926, **£8–10/$13–16**

▲ Blackpool menu
In 1926, a miners' strike led to a general strike when other unions joined the protest. Although this strike collapsed after nine days, the miners protested for a further seven months. In the following year, legislation in the form of the 1927 Trade Disputes and Trade Union Act imposed limits on the right to strike. This divided-back card represents an attempt to raise the spirit of the strikers, and increase public awareness.

World War I

Postcards became the soldiers' main link with their families during this dehumanizing war. These communications were all censored, the true conditions of warfare were concealed, and news from home to the front was also tightly controlled. In France, soldiers bought locally produced "silk postcards", or any other cards they could find, but the most popular cards were the pin-ups. Propaganda cards came into their own, promoting patriotism, confirming the justness of the war, and demonizing the enemy. Newspapers published sets of cards with sanitized images of the front, and pictures of huge new guns, tanks, and aircraft. These were intended to encourage Allied soldiers, and dismay the enemy. The collecting mania for postcards ended with the war, and when stamp prices doubled to one penny, postcard printers began to experience difficult times.

"The Dream – The Reality", postally unused, 1914, **£6–7/$9–11**

▶ **Kaiser Bill**
In the early 20thC European tensions grew for a variety of reasons, including the demand by the German Emperor for "a place in the sun", which gave rise to German colonization in Africa. "Kaiser Bill", as the Emperor was known in British propaganda, was ambitious, vain, and military. This card is from the Patriotic Series, number 2574, produced by PHILCO.

▼ **Rising propaganda**
Gale & Polden, Aldershot, Surrey, best known as a specialist producer of military postcards and pictures for the armed services, frequently commissioned well-known artist Edgar G. Holloway, and there are a number of military sets by him. At this period Germany's military strength, belligerent attitude, and inconsistent foreign policy gave rise to an arms race with Britain. Cards such as the one shown left illustrate the sort of propaganda that prepared Britain for military action. Many political/patriotic cards are available today.

"Where's the blighter who did this?", postally unused, 1914, **£3.50–5/$5.50–8**

Zeppelins (airships)
Many German postcards
from this period show
Zeppelin raids on
English towns, with
people fleeing in terror.
Popular British cards
show the reverse,
with Zeppelins being
destroyed after being
caught in spotlights.

FACT FILE

"The War – The Exodus", postally
unused, c.1914, **£8–10/$13–16**

▲ Belgian experience

The rapid German invasion
in 1914 of Belgium, a small
country unprepared for such
an event, gave rise to long
columns of refugees fleeing
the invading forces. This tinted
photolithoed image of a
family fleeing, with its
possessions on a dog-drawn
cart, demonstrates the plight
of the dispossessed. There are
no publisher's details for this
card except for a Belgian flag
that appears on the front,
bottom left; "LVC" also
appears on
the flag.

▼ German propaganda

This romantic view of life
on the German front line
encouraged enlisting. It was
probably successful, bearing
in mind the appeal of
nationalism to German society
at the time and the conformity
expected from the young. This
artist, Paul Hey (1867–1952),
had an unusually long
working life; his early work
was Art Nouveau style, but it
became more academic later.

"Feuergefecht" (German soldiers
fighting), postally unused, c.1915,
£8–10/$13–16

▼ Military themes

Cards such as the one below,
produced by Gale & Polden
and printed in Britain, were
published by companies
specializing in military themes.
This one was produced at the
time of Britain's entry into the
war. Britain and France had
disagreed over the conduct
of the Boer War, and, during
the Russo-Japanese War, over
British support for Japan
against Russia, an ally of
France. Now, however, the
three countries (Britain,
France, and Russia) were
united to face a common
enemy – Germany.

"Now we are alright", postally
unused, c.1914, **£3–5/$5–8**

"Guerre de 1914–15", postally unused, **£4–5/$6–8**

▲ German plane forced down

This postcard depicts a German "Aviatik" reconnaisance biplane, probably the "B1". It had two seats, a Mercedes six-cylinder engine, 100hp capable of 62mph, and a wingspan of 13.97m (45ft 10in). The public was anxious to know any details of aircraft or armaments, and the postcard was the main source of information. The Allied authorities were more evasive about details of their aircraft. This French photographic card is by L'H Paris.

▼ Bombed houses

Although at first the USA resisted involvement in a European war, the sinking by U-boats of passenger liners in 1915 made it more sympathetic to the Allies' cause. Subsequently, in April 1917, after Germany had attempted to gain Mexico's support, the USA became fully involved in the war. This card, photographed by "LL", produced in collotype by Lévy Fils et cie, Paris, shows a group of Americans viewing war damage. Despite the devastation, Lévy's composition is interesting.

"Well, if you knows of a better 'ole, go to it."

"Well, if you knows of a better 'ole ...", postally unused, 1916, **£4–6/$6–9**

▲ Eyewitness

This is probably the most famous of Bruce Bairnsfather's illustrations, which originated in sketches he made during the two years he spent in the trenches. Although he was wounded at Ypres, Bairnsfather continued to draw, and drawings he made were published in *The Tatler* and *Bystander* magazines; the latter then reproduced them as postcards, issued as eight sets of six cards each. The black humour that characterizes these cards succeeds in giving us some insight into the horror of World War I.

"American Mission at the Calvary", postally unused, 1915–16, **£1–1.50/ $1.60–2.50**

"Souvenir from France", postally used, 1916, **£2–2.50/$3–4**

▲ Silk cards

Before the war, forerunners to cards such as this silk-embroidered one featured elaborate machine-woven pictures; the best known of these were produced by Stevens and Grant. During the war a cottage industry produced these rather "primitive" cards, the colour and design of which reflected the raw emotions of men trying to express their feelings to their loved ones at home. Some "silks" show regimental badges, and battle honours, but these are less common today.

Photograph of soldier, postally unused, 1917, **£2–2.50/$3–4**

▼ "Real photo" cards

This is a good example of a "real photo" postcard, which was taken for the soldier's sister (see signed front). Clearly, this is a battle-weary soldier whose picture has been taken by a provincial photographer, in a moment of respite. It speaks volumes about the misery of the times through which such men lived. Sadly, the next picture in the album from which this picture was taken is that of a gravestone.

"The Language of Stamps", postally used, 1918, **£3–5/$5–8**

▲ Wartime novelty card

Even in the misery of war, there was time for humour, and this is a wartime adaptation of a pre-war novelty card produced by Inter Art, London, Comique series number 2314. It is in the same vein as "The language of flowers", "The language of fruit", and even "The language of noses"! For weary correspondents unable to express themselves freely on a postcard because of censorship, it was useful to have a private code to add an extra message.

Between the wars

After World War I, a desire for reform was widespread. In the USA, change came about through the huge influx of immigrants bringing new skills and vitality, but in Europe it was not achieved so smoothly.

The public's attitude to postcards changed: there was no longer the variety available; postage costs, and the cost of the cards themselves, rose, and the telephone became more common as a means of communication. Newspapers and magazines also improved in reproduction, and they assumed much of the postcard's reportage role. The postcard's repertoire was reduced to the mainly scenic, commemorative, comic, "art", glamour, birthday, and advertising, and quality was not always high. The postcard was, however, far from finished.

▼ **Mechanical novelties**
This card was published during the "Roaring '20s", a time when people were determined to put the war behind them and enjoy themselves. Dressed in Art Deco fashion, the couple on this card move from side to side, as a lever is moved, in a simple, but effective simulation of the Charleston. As well as producing this card, E.T.W. Dennis & Sons Ltd, London and Scarborough, also manufactured a number of novelty pop-up and pull-out versions.

"Doing the Charleston", postally unused, c.1920, **£8–10/$13–16**

Doing the Charleston.

▼ **Mailing novelties**
Published as a "Mailing novelty" by Valentine & Sons, this card shows an early valve wireless (radio) with a trumpet loudspeaker, and headphones on a front flap that conceals pull-out views of London. The heading refers to "2LO", the call sign of the British Broadcasting Company Ltd. It became a public body, and was renamed the British Broadcasting Corporation in 1926.

"Hello! Hello! London Calling", postally used, 1926, **£12–15/$20–24**

Hello! Hello!! LONDON Calling

▼ Solo flight

Charles A. Lindbergh became an international hero when, on 21 May 1927, he flew his Ryan/Mahoney aeroplane solo across the Atlantic from New York to Paris, thereby winning $25,000. The potential implications for safe and reliable transport by air immediately created a rush for aircraft industry stocks. Lindbergh toured Britain and other European countries before returning to the USA as a celebrity. This commemorative card was produced and printed in France in collotype by "Edit. Farineau".

"Lindbergh", postally unused, 1927, **£15–20/$24–32**

▲ Plane racing

Public interest in car and aircraft racing grew enormously between the wars. The cut-throat competition between the industrialized nations that resulted from such races had increasingly political overtones. The aeroplane depicted on this card, the precursor of the "Spitfire", won the 1927 Schneider Trophy Race at Venice. This card was painted and signed by the artist Leonard Bridgman.

▼ Trade promotion

Printed on thick card, this poster-like card has a bold, Art Deco-style image. Unfortunately, the artist is not credited, but he has created an assured piece of graphic work. The Empire Marketing Board was an efficient enterprise that promoted strong trading links between the various countries comprising the British Empire. This card was produced by the Empire Marketing Board, P.C.T3, and printed in England by Hudson & Kearns Ltd.

"John Bull, Sons & Daughters, Ltd – Empire Fruiterers", postally unused, 1928, **£14–15/$22–24**

▼ Cartoon cards

Felix, the most popular cartoon character of the silent-film era, was designed by Otto Mesmer for the Pat Sullivan Studio. Mesmer developed Felix's animation through the study of short films by Charles Chaplin. In 1919, he worked for Sullivan on "Feline Follies", in which Felix made his debut for Paramount. By 1925, through Sullivan's promotion and Mesmer's animation, Felix was globally successful. A card featuring a cricket-playing Felix is likely to have been one made specially for the UK market. On the back of this card is: "Felix the Film Cat, which appears exclusively in Pathé's Eve and Everybody's Film Review".

"Felix the Cat", postally unused, 1928, **£14–15/$22–24**

"You saucy little witches …", postally used, 1932, **£4–6/$6–9**

▲ Seaside cards

This seaside card shows a confident generation of modern women at play wearing fashionable "Beach Pyjamas" with bold, Art Deco patterns. The artist, Reg Maurice, was very prolific, and he produced many cards for the Regent Publishing company, usually with a colour frame around the picture. This card throws an interesting sidelight on how the role of postcards had changed – it is overstamped "The Telephone makes Life Easy".

▼ Commemorative card

The 1936 Olympic Games were used by Hitler as a showcase for his triumphalist Nazi regime. A film of the event, called "Triumph of the Will", glorified the so-called "Aryan Ideal". When the black US athlete Jesse Owens won four gold medals, Hitler, furious at having his racial theories compromised, refused to meet him. Most cards from this period were lost during the war, but since the reunification of Germany cards such as this are available, and highly sought after.

Olympics 1936, postally used, (with pre-printed stamp and special Olympics stamp) **£15–18/$24–30**; unstamped **£10–12/$16–19**

▼ News distribution

Produced by Valentine & Sons, this "real photograph" card bears an inscription on the address side: "Prints flown to Dundee by Aeroplane on Coronation Day, May 12th, 1937. Postcards on sale in London by 11 o'clock on 13th May." This suggests, first, that there was competition between postcards and newspapers as news distributors, and, second, that despite the constitutional problems raised by the abdication of Edward VIII, members of the royal family were still regarded with affection. Cards of royalty are less popular today, and are consequently cheaper.

"Coronation Souvenir", postally unused, 1937, **£4–6/$6–9** (for an exceptional card; normally **£1.50–2/$2.50–3**)

"Ginger Rogers and Fred Astaire", postally unused, 1936, **£6–8/$9–13**

▲ Cinema stars

Although in the 1930s most countries were producing their owns films, Hollywood was still the dominant force, helped by the many emigrants who, fleeing the political convulsions engulfing Europe, had settled there. They brought a rich variety of talent, and helped create films with world-wide appeal. Astaire and Rogers are examples of the stars that appeared in such films. Cards of 1930s stars are more expensive than cards of their silent-film counterparts. This tinted, photographic-print card was produced by Art Photo.

Thought provoking

The horrors of the Spanish Civil War demonstrated the ruthlessness of undemocratic regimes, and cards from this period, both pro- and anti-fascist, reflect the increasing international alarm such events provoked. These cards are now very collectable.

"Heil Gran'pop", postally unused, 1938, **£10–12/$16–20**

▲ Political humour

The humour of this card reflects an attitude towards German politics and Hitler similar to that of the Chaplin film *The Great Dictator*. The film was highly controversial, and no doubt this card also offended many. We can now appreciate how farsighted they were in alerting the unwary to the dangers of totalitarian regimes. This card was by Valentine's Lawson Wood.

World War II

Britain adopted austerity and rationing in order to survive in World War II. Everything was in short supply. Postcard printers, when paper was available, turned their main effort to morale-building and propaganda. Many old albums of cards were pulped for the war effort, and new cards were utilitarian. Enthusiasm for the postcard in Europe also waned. However, the lack of wartime cards makes those that survive more interesting, and an absorbing picture of wartime life can be pieced together from them. The sophisticated advertising industry in the USA threw its power behind the campaign when the Americans too became involved in the war, and excellent cards from this period exist.

▼ V for Victory

Although the reclining lady trademark is missing from this unusual, lithographed card, produced by Raphael Tuck & Sons Ltd, which is a wartime special, it does have the customary Royal Warrant and Easel logo. The bold "V for Victory" that Churchill made his trademark appears on the card, combined with the opening notes of Beethoven's Fifth Symphony. The card was clearly a morale booster, and examples were doubtless seen in offices, homes, and barrack-rooms alike.

Tuck's postcard for Victory, postally unused, c.1942, **£10–12/ $16–20**

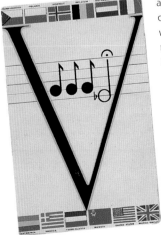

▼ Social history

In 1939, when war became inevitable, the Britain's Civil Defence encouraged parents to send their children from cities to temporary, safe homes in the country. This unusual card shows children being evacuated from Catford in south east London: note the identifying labels attached to the children and their luggage, and a barrage balloon in the background. No producer or printer is credited for this "real photograph" card.

Evacuees, postally unused, 1940, **£20–25/ $32–40**

Normandy
Landings, arrival
of Allied
reinforcements,
postally unused,
c.1945,
£8–10/$13–16

Information cards
The postcard played an
important part in WWII,
by both boosting morale
and disseminating
important government
information. Advice on
maintaining blackout
control, for example,
was publicized in a
series of cards, published
by Raphael Tuck, simply
called "Black-out".

▼ Humorous propaganda

Produced by Bamforth & Co,
Holmfirth, England, as a
"War-time Greeting", this
card constitutes a piece
of humorous, wartime
propaganda aimed at
maintaining civilian morale.
Germany, in attempting to cut
Britain's supply routes, was
unable to inflict significant
damage with its cruisers,
but made deadly use of
its U-boats. Despite massive
maritime losses, it was still
necessary for Britain to bring
vital materials and supplies
into the country by
sea, while
supplying
Russia
with war
materials
by way
of North
Atlantic
convoys.

U-Boats,
postally
unused, c.1943,
£8–10/$13–16

▲ US landings

Published by Editions Gaby
Artaud, père et fils, Editeurs,
Nantes, this wonderful, "real
photograph" card shows the
arrival of US forces in France.
It is one of a series, and was
printed shortly after the
event. The Allied forces,
under the command of
General Eisenhower, landed
in northern France on 6 June
1944. They had taken
Cherbourg by 30 June, after
which they began to work
their way towards Paris.

▼ Celebrating victory

Printed in France, this card
was lithographed and signed
by the artist, M. Falter. It
appears to be part of a series
celebrating the Allied forces'
victory in Europe. The flags
of Russia, the USA, Britain,
and France hang together,
with, in the background, the
Statue of Liberty. The German
armed forces surrendered to
General Eisenhower on 7 May
1945, and, on 8 May, they
repeated this capitulation at
the headquarters of the Soviet
forces. World War II cards,
such as this, are scarce, and
interest in them is increasing.

Jeep with Allied flags, postally
unused, 1945, **£8–10/$13–16**

Icons & celebrities

The cult status accorded to celebrities usually generates a wealth of collectable memorabilia, much of which is instantly destroyed when the fashionable look loses favour, or when the celebrity holds no appeal for the next generation. For this reason, items that survive, such as postcards of famous people, are likely to increase in value in the future.

The collecting of postcards of a specific icon can lead to a fascinating and absorbing collection, in which frequently unrecognized facets of the celebrity's career are recorded. As with all themes, collect only material that interests you personally – your intuition will be the best guide – so that if your collection gives you pleasure, its commercial value is only of secondary importance.

Marlon Brando, postally unused, c.1984, **50p–£1/ 80c–$1.50**

▼ **Marlon Brando**
Born in 1924, Brando came from the stage to the cinema in the early 1950s as a leading proponent of the method school of acting. His reputation is based on appearances in *A Streetcar Named Desire* and *On the Waterfront* and, later, *The Godfather*, *Last Tango in Paris*, and *Apocalypse Now*. Although there are umpteen cards based on Brando's screen career, those from his stage appearances, and those taken under other circumstances, are much harder to come by, and are more collectable.

▶ **Marilyn Monroe**
This Marilyn collage postcard is by Elisabeth Broel, Cologne, Germany. Marilyn Monroe (1926–62) is one of the best-known and most loved cinema icons of all time. She appeared first in the early 1950s in "dumb blonde" roles; her reputation is founded on films such as *The Seven Year Itch* and *Some Like It Hot*. A collection of cards showing all aspects of Monroe's career would plot the creation of a 20thC equivalent of a goddess.

Marilyn Monroe, postally unused, 1981, **60p–£1/ $1–1.50**

Icons

Cards of older groups or established artists are often reproductions. It is best to go to dealers specializing in earlier periods, and look for publishers such as Gary Cards, Valex, Nems, Brel, Classico, and Pomegranate.

▼ Elvis Presley

Elvis Presley in uniform, printed by Metro Music, depicts the early rock star whose life assumed legendary proportions. His influence on the popular music of his time was immense. Huge numbers of cards were produced, all reflecting different aspects of Presley's career, including his service in the US Army. As with other stars whose careers span decades, a collection of cards would show the build-up to his universal popularity with the changes that occurred over a lengthy period of time.

Elvis Presley, postally unused, c.1980, **60p–£1/$1–1.50**

▼ James Dean

A star whose reputation is based on leading roles in only three films, Dean was highly influential during his short film career. Dean's tragic and untimely death in a car crash ensured his cinematic immortality. There are many cards of this star on and off screen. Although a collection of cards featuring this artist is likely to be modest compared to others, it would certainly make a fascinating group.

James Dean, postally unused, c.1977, **60p–£1/$1–1.50**

▼ The Beatles

This legendary Liverpool pop group comprised George Harrison, (Sir) Paul McCartney, John Lennon, and Ringo Starr. The group's highly original music helped change the pop music industry forever; it also contributed to our picture of the "Swinging Sixties". The group split up in 1971, and John Lennon was shot dead in New York in 1980. A representative collection of cards would show the group, each member, and examples of their publicity stunts, and their films.

The Beatles, postally unused; the original is 1967, but this is a later reproduction by the US Postcard Company Inc., **60p–£1/$1–1.50**

Modern times

The richest period for postcards was 1900–20, and it remains the most popular with collectors. Nevertheless, subsequent periods are likely to yield many cards of interest to the perceptive collector. This is also true for cards currently in production, which are likely to be of nostalgic and historical interest in the future. Movements that have changed society, for example, such as the Thatcher years, can be documented from published cards. This is also true of icons, such as Diana, Princess of Wales, where the public's changing attitude towards her, and royalty in general, are evident. There is a rich mixture, still being documented, of cards dealing with social history, sport, and cinema, as well as art and advertising cards.

"reconstruire l'europe", postally unused, 1947, **£5–7/$8–11**

▶ **European recovery**
This is a historically interesting card: the design by Alban Wijss won the prize in a poster competition to publicize "the Marshall Plan". It was probably a public relations exercise to boost morale after the war. In 1947, the US Secretary of State, George Marshall, proposed the European Recovery Programme, under which the USA supplied raw materials, goods, and capital, partly as credit, partly as direct subsidy. This jump-started the economies of participating countries, such as The Netherlands.

▼ **Sputnik anniversary**
With the collapse of the former USSR, postcard collectors and dealers are able to move more readily between countries. As a result, there has been an influx into the West of many interesting cards, and these are likely to provide a stimulus to new collectors. Such a card is shown below – it celebrates Soviet space achievements, in this case a Sputnik anniversary card, with a special stamp, and overstamping for the occasion. The named artist is Lesegerics.

"The Pioneer of the Space Age", postally unused, 1962, **£12–15/ $20–24**

"He's safer than a wolf", postally used, 1977, **£6–8/$9–13**

FACT FILE

Definitions
Here is a useful guide to grouping cards after 1950, devised by Pete Davies, who compiled *Collect Modern Postcards* (see *What to read*, p.60):

Early modern
(1950–80)
Modern
(1981–1994)
Contemporary
(1995–)

▼ Photographers

The variety of photographic cards available today is enormous. Photographic publishers, such as Fotofolia, Athena, and Art Unlimited, feature images by numerous photographers. And photographic collections, such as the Hulton-Getty, publish archival photographs. It is quite easy to collect the work of a single photographer, such as Don McCullin. Such cards can give an insight into the career of the photographer, in this case Ken Griffiths, and are rewarding to collect, whether or not the photographer becomes famous.

"Enquiries", postally unused, 1974, **£1–2/$1.50–3**

▲ 1950s glamour

The card above is an excellent example of '50s over-the-top glamour artwork – glamour with a twinkle in its eye. Since there are five similar paintings by glamour artists of the "Vargas" school, this Mutascope card is likely to be one of a set of six. Its character as "showbizzy" fun, or light entertainment, would make it attractive to many collectors, but it would also appeal to collectors of circus cards.

"Harmful", postally unused, c.1980, **£2–3/$3–5**

▲ Social comment

John Stalin (aka John Churchill) has been producing postcards since 1978, and many of his early sets have been out of print for some years. Such cards are popular, and their brand of humour and social comment, mixed with striking imagery, makes a wonderful collection. The coarse texture of images, which results from repeated copying, is characteristic. This artist has also worked for the music and film industries.

American Gothic, postally used, 1981, **£3–4/$5–6**

"Fresh Fruit/Rock Hudson", postally unused, 1980, **£3–4/$5–6**

▲ **Xeroxed cards**
Chic Pix of London experimented with the new colour Xerox machines in its early postcards, which appeared in 1980. Like many card publishers of the time, the company discovered it could by-pass traditional printing methods with the new processes. Its early images were collages of popular film stars and ephemera, treated in Pop Art style, colour-copied, and spray-mounted onto card, but such a labour-intensive operation limited its output. The company was still producing series such as "London–Style City" in 1986.

PICASSO

"Picasso-Circle", postally unused, 1981, **£2–3/$3–5**

▲ **Visual puns**
This is part of a visually witty set of four cards produced by Millimetre Ltd, London. In 1990 the company changed its name to Paradise Lost, but it was unfortunately dissolved shortly afterwards although cards that it produced are available. Cards produced by companies that flourish briefly before disappearing frequently have a scarcity value. This minimalist card was designed by Emmanuel and Erofili.

▲ **Anti-establishment**
The American Postcard Company, founded around 1980, earned the reputation for witty, anti-establishment postcards, in which all aspects of US life, politics, and social mores received its attention. It has a wide range of "Alternative Miss America"-type glamour postcards, together with cards on animals, films, TV, and pop culture. Hot Lava is a subsidiary company, specializing in comic (rude) cards. Cards that feature US presidents always attract interest from collectors.

"Greetings at the speed of light",
postally unused, 1981,
£2–3/$3–5

▲ Sci-fi treatment

Little information is available
on the British group that
produced this card – Bunch
of Artists/Flip it – active in the
1990s. Its working methods
seem similar to those of John
Stalin (see page 55), in which
xeroxed or coloured images,
or materials found at random,
were juxtaposed with other
images to make bizarre or
amusing collages. Cards were
then printed conventionally,
and usually varnished. Series
on the cinema, politics,
UK royalty,
and transport
were produced.

▼ Cigarette advertisements

Camden Graphics appeared in
the late 1970s, and, although
postcards were only a small
part of its output, the
company produced some
excellent, collectable sets.
These sets, although printed
in relatively large numbers,
are now comparatively scarce.
The Benson & Hedges set,
an example of which is
shown below, is imaginative,
and deservedly popular
with collectors.

Flying ducks, postally unused,
1982, **£2–3/$3–5**

▼ Biff cards

The creation of Mick Kidd and
Chris Garrett, Biff cards are
characterized by their wit and
off-the-wall humour. The first
cards appeared in the early
1980s; new designs have
since been added, and old
ones been dropped. There
have been some 200 designs
since their first appearance.
The Biff cartoon strip appears
in the UK's *The Guardian*
newspaper every Saturday.

"Yuppie Love", postally used,
1987, **50p–£1.50/80c–$2.50**

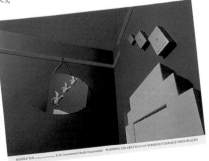

"Stockmarket Crash", postally used, 1987, **£1–2/$1.50–3**

"Yes ... but do the poor ...", postally unused, c.1987, **£1–1.50/$1.50–2.50**

▲ Topical cards

Leeds Postcards is a company started in 1979 by Richard Scott. He started publishing political postcards as a hobby, but within two years this had turned into a full-time enterprise. The company's huge range of cards covers topics such as politics, social issues and campaigns (unions, feminism, and world peace), and topical events. Famous artists and cartoonists, such as Steve Bell and Gerald Scarfe, have contributed to a catalogue of cards which is stimulating and motivated. The card above is by Ian Hering.

▲ Postcard magazines

This card's artist, Anne Rusnak, worked from her home in Carson City, Nevada, USA. Postcards were her great hobby, and she helped pioneer US interest in modern postcards by publishing the *Nevada Checklist* and *Postcard Examiner* magazines, and series of cards on topical events, politics, and social issues. Sometimes printing her own cards by hand (like this one), she produced many cards for postcard fairs, worked for British and French publishers, and appeared as "visiting artist" at the 1994 Centenary Picture Postcard Show, London.

▼ "Cult" anti-establishment

Steve Hardstaff and Rick Walker were based in Manchester, England, around 1982, when they created South Atlantic Souvenir (SAS) postcards. Frustrated by the lack of public protest at the Falklands War, they produced their most famous series. Their cards reflect a radical, alternative view of life, covering both politics and social issues. They produced what is probably the first Aids awareness postcard, "Be my Valentine", which imaginatively shows two deep-sea divers in full protective gear. This is an example of their impressive, feisty, and highly collectable Christmas card series. (Also of interest to collectors of royal memorabilia.)

"All I want for Christmas is ..." postally unused, c.1989, **£2–3/$3–5**

Dog in collar and tie, postally
unused, 1985, **£2–3/$3–5**

▲ Pooch cards

At the turn of the 19thC,
publishers issued limited
editions of new cards on
special cardboard, with gold
edges, which were more
expensive than the standard
cards they subsequently
released. Current practice is
to limit the total print run of
a card, and to release it at an
increased price. Such cards
have a scarcity value. The
card shown, Connolly's Dumb
Animals series, limited edition
3000, is a British artist's card.

▼ Barbie doll

The card below represents
yet another ironic dig at the
consumer society. Think what
you will of her, Barbie is an
extraordinary phenomenon.
"Born" in 1959, and named
after Mattel founders Ruth
and Elliot Handler's little
girl, the doll is described
by her biographers as "the
embodiment of the collective
consciousness of America". In
1992, the average American
child owned seven Barbies,
with innumerable accessories.

"Thought of you",
postally unused, c.1990,
50p–£1/80c–$1.50

R.M. Williams' boots, postally
unused, 1999, **40–60p/60c–$1**

▲ Free postcards

Since the 1980s, free
postcards have proliferated.
Although the quality of many
of the unsolicited, direct-mail
cards is poor, clever specimens
are worth collecting from racks
in many restaurants and shops.
These are usually well-designed,
with intriguing imagery and
eye-catching graphics.

What to read

Barker, Ronnie *Book of Boudoir Beauties* (Hodder & Stoughton, London, 1975)

Byatt, Anthony *Picture Postcards & Their Publishers* (Golden Age Postcard Books, Malvern, Worcs, 1978)

Bonynge, Richard *A Collector's Guide to Theatrical Postcards* (Grange Books, London, 1993)

Bowers, Felicity *Greetings from Bath* (Kingsmead Press, Bath, 1986)

Buckland, Elfreda *The World of Donald McGill* (Blandford Press, Poole, Dorset, reprinted 1990)

Carline, Richard *Pictures in the Post, The Story of the Picture Postcard* (Gordon Fraser, London, 1971)

Calder-Marshall, Arthur *The Art of Donald McGill* (Hutchinson, London, 1966 2nd imprint)

Cope, Dawn & Peter *Illustrators of Postcards from the Nursery* (East-West Publications, London, 1978)

Coysh, A.W. *The Dictionary of Picture Postcards in Britain 1894–1939* (Antique Collectors' Club, Woodbridge, Suffolk, 1996)

Curtis, Tony *Printed Collectables/Lyle Price Guide* (Lyle Publications, Scotland, 1990)

Davies, Pete *Collect Modern Postcards vols 1, 2, & 3* (Reflections of a Bygone Age, Nottingham, 1998)

Duval, William with Monahan, Valerie *Collecting Postcards 1894–1914* (Blandford Press, Poole, Dorset, 1978)

Fanelli, Giovanni & Godoli, Ezio *Collecting Picture Postcards* (Phaidon-Christie's, Oxford, 1987)

Godden, Geoffrey *Collecting Picture Postcards* (Phillimore, Chichester, West Sussex, 1996)

Hammond, Paul *French Undressing/Naughty Postcards from 1900 to 1920* (Jupiter Books, London, 1976)

Holt, Tonie & Valmai *Picture Postcards of the Golden Age* (MacGibbon& Kee, London, 1971)

Holt, Tonie & Valmai *Till the Boys Come Home: Postcards of the First World War* (Macdonald and James, London, 1977)

Howell, Georgina *The Penguin Book of Naughty Postcards* (Penguin, London, 1977)

Klamkin, Marian *Picture Postcards* (David & Charles, Newton Abbot, Devon, 1974)

Lauterbach, C. & Jakovsky, A. *A Picture Postcard Album* (Thames and Hudson, London, 1961)

Mashburn, J.L. *The Postcard Price Guide* (Colonial House, North Carolina, 1997)

Morgan and Brown *Prairie Fires and Paper Moons. The American Photographic Postcard: 1900–1920* (Godine, Boston)

Smith, J.H.D. *Picture postcard Values 1999* (IPM, Colchester, Essex, 1999)

Walvin, James *Beside the Seaside* (Allen Lane, Penguin Books Ltd, 1978)

Welsch, Roger L. *Tell-Tale Postcards* (A.S. Barnes and Co. Inc., New Jersey; Thomas Yoseloff Ltd, London, 1976)

Whitney, Dr J.T. *Collect British Postmarks* (Author, Benfleet, Essex, 1979)

Willoughby, Martin *Postcards* (Phillips Collectors Guides, Boxtree, London, 1989)

Where to buy

POSTCARD AUCTIONS, FAIRS, AND SALES

Acorn Auctions
PO Box 152
Salford M17 1SD
tel: 0161 877 8818

The Autumn South of England Postcard Fair
Woking Leisure Centre
King Field Road
Woking GU22 9BA
tel: 01483 771122

Bloomsbury Postcard & Collectors' Fair
Royal National Hotel
Bedford Way
London WC1H 0DG
tel: 020 8202 9080

Corinium Galleries
25 Gloucester Street
Cirencester GL7 2DJ
tel: 01285 659057
fax: 01285 652047

Dalkeith Auctions
Dalkeith Hall
Dalkeith Steps
Rear 81 Old Christchurch Road
Bournemouth BH1 1YL
tel: 01202 292905

Postcard and Paper Collectors' Fair
Twickenham Rugby Ground
Rugby Road
Twickenham TW1 1DZ
tel: 020 8892 5712

Postcard Show
Royal Horticultural Hall
80 Vincent Square
London SW1P 2PE
tel: 020 7821 3075

South of England Postcard Fair
Guildford Civic Hall
London Road
Guildford GU1 2AA
tel: 01483 444555
fax: 01483 301982

Specialized Postcard Auctions
25 Gloucester Street
Cirencester GL7 2DJ
tel: 01285 659057

York Card Expo
York Race Course
York YO23 1EX
tel: 01904 620911

DEALERS

Memories
130 Brent Street
London NW4 2DR
tel: 020 8203 1500
fax: 020 8203 7031

Moderns
Brighton Postcard Shop
38 Beaconsfield Road
Brighton BN1 4QH

R F Postcards
17 Hilary Crescent
Rayleigh SS6 8NB
tel: 01268 794886

WEBSITES
The internet is now a market site for finding postcards for sale, and sites should be explored, albeit with caution as to condition of postcards.

www.collectors.org/calendar
A list of postcard fairs.

www.vintagepostcards.com
Offers vintage postcards. It will do searches and also has online archives.

www.deltiology.org
Postcard collecting worldwide, including links to specialist dealers.

www.thepostcard.com
Antique, collectable, and modern postcards for sale.

www.playle.com
Online postcard auctions.

www.cool-card.com
A specialist postcard site.

OTHER USEFUL ADDRESSES
Picture Postcard Monthly
tel: 0115 937 4079

The Postcard Club of Great Britain
c/o Mrs D Brennan
34 Harper House
St James's Crescent
London SW9 7LW
tel: 020 7771 9404

Index

Acknowledgments

The author would like to thank the following for their help and advice on this project:
Ed Smith, Raymond Notley, Ethan Ames and Michael Goldsmith.

Photographic acknowledgments
Mary Evans Picture Library 43 t, 50 r
Octopus Publishing Group Ltd/A. J. Photographics/Chris Connor 1, 2, 5, 6 t, 6 b, 7, 8 t, 8 b, 9 t, 9 c, 10 tl, 10 tr, 10 b, 11 t, 11 bl, 11 br, 12 t, 12 b, 13 t, 13 c, 13 b, 14 t, 14 bl, 14 br, 15 t, 15 bl, 15 br, 16 l, 16 r, 17 t, 17 bl, 17 br, 18 t, 18 bl, 18 br, 19 t, 19 bl, 19 br, 20 t, 20 b, 21 t, 21 bl, 21 br, 22 l, 22 r, 23 l, 23 r, 23 c, 24 l, 24 r, 25 l, 25 c, 25 r, 26 l, 26 r, 27 t, 27 c, 27 b, 28 l, 28 r, 29 t, 29 bl, 29 br, 30 t, 30 b, 31 t, 31 bl, 31 br, 32 r, 32 t, 33 t, 33 c, 33 b, 34 l, 34 r, 35 t, 35 bl, 35 br, 36 t, 36 b, 37 t, 37 c, 37 b, 38 t, 38 b, 39 t, 39 bl, 39 br, 40 l, 40 r, 41 tl, 41 tr, 41 b, 42 t, 42 b, 43 bl, 43 br, 44 tl, 44 tr, 44 b, 45 t, 45 c, 45 b, 46 l, 47 t, 47 bl, 47 br, 48 t, 48 bl, 48 br, 49 c, 50 l, 51 t, 51 bl, 51 br, 52 l, 52 r, 53 l, 53 c, 53 br, 54 t, 54 b, 55 t, 55 c, 55 b, 56 l, 56 r, 56 c, 57 t, 57 bl, 57 br, 58 tl, 58 tr, 58 b, 59 l, 59 r, 59 b, /Memories 46 r, 49 t, 49 b

---

Prices
The price ranges given in this book should be taken as guides to value only, as value depends greatly on trends in the market place, geographical locations, and condition.